The Amazing Afri

Cookbook

50 Flavorful African Recipes to Delight You and Your

Family

BY: SOPHIA FREEMAN

COPYRIGHTED

Liability

This publication is meant as an informational tool. The individual purchaser accepts all liability if damages occur because of following the directions or guidelines set out in this publication. The Author bears no responsibility for reparations caused by the misuse or misinterpretation of the content.

Copyright

The content of this publication is solely for entertainment purposes and is meant to be purchased by one individual. Permission is not given to any individual who copies, sells or distributes parts or the whole of this publication unless it is explicitly given by the Author in writing.

Table of Contents

Introduction

It's true that there are not too many African restaurants around the world.

It's also true that African cuisine is not as popular as French, Italian, Indian, or Chinese fare.

But this doesn't mean that African cuisine should be ignored.

It's actually very rich and vibrant. It's more remarkable than most people realize.

African cuisine is known for its emphasis on clean and natural eating, balanced diet, and aromatic flavors.

It's also known for its use of herbs and spices.

Now that you have this book, you can explore the wide array of African dishes that will surely fill your kitchen with delicious aroma and flavors.

For sure, you're going to have so much fun.

So, are you ready to get started?

Lamb Tagine

Tagine refers to a dish that originated in North Africa. It is typically made of braised spiced meat. In this recipe, we slow cook the lamb, barley, apricots and cinnamon, and garnish with raisins and cilantro. It is one African dish that certainly doesn't fall short on flavors, colors, and textures.

Serving Size: 8

Preparation Cooking Time: 8 hours and 30 minutes

Ingredients:

- 2 onions, chopped
- 2 tablespoons cloves garlic, minced
- 1 cup uncooked barley (preferably whole grain)
- 6 oz. dried apricot halves
- 3 cups beef stock (unsalted)
- 3 tablespoons tomato paste
- 1 ½ teaspoons ground cumin
- 2 cinnamon sticks
- ½ teaspoon cayenne pepper
- 1 teaspoon ground coriander
- Salt to taste
- 2 lb. lamb shoulder, fat trimmed and sliced into cubes
- 1 tablespoon freshly squeezed lemon juice
- ½ cup golden raisins
- ½ cup fresh cilantro leaves, chopped

Instructions:

1. Combine the onion, garlic, barley, apricot, beef stock, tomato paste, cumin, cinnamon sticks, cayenne pepper, ground coriander and salt in the slow cooker.

2. Place your pan over medium high heat.

3. Brown the lamb cubes for 6 to 8 minutes.

4. Transfer the lamb to the slow cooker.

5. Cover the pot.

6. Cook on low for 8 hours.

7. Remove the cinnamon sticks.

8. Stir in the lemon juice, raisins and cilantro before serving.

Nutrients per Serving:

- Calories 436
- Fat 18 g
- Saturated fat 7 g
- Carbohydrates 43 g
- Fiber 8 g
- Protein 27 g
- Cholesterol 14 mg
- Sugars 18 g
- Sodium 647 mg
- Potassium 550 mg

Moroccan Chicken Tagine

Have fun preparing this Moroccan chicken tagine dish overflowing with luscious flavors thanks to the aromatic spice mixture called ras el hanout. If you can't find it in the supermarket, you can replace it with a mixture of ground cumin, ground ginger, ground cinnamon, allspice, and coriander.

Serving Size: 6

Preparation Cooking Time: 40 minutes

Ingredients:

- 1 lb. chicken thigh, sliced into small pieces
- Salt to taste
- 2 tablespoons olive oil, divided
- 1 onion, chopped
- 1 tablespoon fresh ginger, grated
- 1 tablespoon garlic, crushed and minced
- 1 teaspoon lemon zest
- 2 teaspoons ras el hanout
- 1 tablespoon tomato paste
- 15 oz. chickpeas, rinsed and drained
- 2 cups chicken broth (unsalted)
- ½ cup green olives, pitted and sliced in half
- ½ cup dried apricots, chopped
- ½ cup almonds, toasted, slivered and divided
- Fresh cilantro leaves, chopped
- 1 tablespoon lemon juice

Instructions:

1. Season the chicken with the salt.

2. Pour half of the olive oil into a pan over medium heat.

3. Cook the chicken for 2 to 3 minutes per side or until brown.

4. Transfer to a plate.

5. Pour the remaining oil into the pan.

6. Add the onion and cook for 4 minutes.

7. Stir in the ginger, garlic, lemon zest, ras el hanout and tomato paste.

8. Cook while stirring for 30 seconds.

9. Add the chickpeas, broth, olives, dried apricots and half of the almonds.

10. Put the chicken back to the pan.

11. Bring to a boil.

12. Reduce heat and simmer for 8 to 10 minutes.

13. Stir in the lemon juice.

14. Season with the salt.

15. Top with the remaining almonds and fresh cilantro before serving.

Nutrients per Serving:

- Calories 344

- Fat 16.8 g

- Saturated fat 2.7 g

- Carbohydrates 26.9 g

- Fiber 5.9 g

- Protein 21.5 g

- Cholesterol 50 mg

- Sugars 11 g

- Sodium 473 mg

- Potassium 579 mg

Hawawshi

Hawawshi, a popular street food in Cairo, Egypt, is a sandwich stuffed with ground beef, veggies, spices and herbs, made using a Panini press.

Serving Size: 8

Preparation Cooking Time: 35 minutes

Ingredients:

- 1 onion, sliced into wedges
- 1 tomato, sliced
- 1 Italian hot pepper
- 1 green bell pepper
- Salt and pepper to taste
- ½ teaspoon ground allspice
- 3 tablespoons fresh cilantro, chopped
- 2 lb. lean ground beef
- 4 whole-wheat pita, sliced in half

Instructions:

1. Add the onion, tomato, hot pepper and bell pepper in the food processor.

2. Pulse until chopped.

3. Season with the salt, pepper and allspice.

4. Transfer the onion and tomato mixture to a bowl.

5. Stir in the cilantro and beef.

6. Spread the mixture on top of the pita half.

7. Top with the other pita half.

8. Preheat your panini press.

9. Press the sandwiches for 5 minutes or until golden and crispy.

Nutrients per Serving:

- Calories 346
- Fat 11.5 g
- Saturated fat 4.1 g
- Carbohydrates 25.7 g
- Fiber 3.1 g
- Protein 35.2 g
- Cholesterol 87 mg
- Sugars 2 g
- Sodium 605 mg
- Potassium 530 mg

Lentil Soup

This lentil soup can be made using brown, yellow, or red lentils. Don't use black or green as these are not soft enough to be pureed.

Serving Size: 8

Preparation Cooking Time: 1 hour

Ingredients:

- 1 tablespoon sunflower oil
- ¼ cup onion, sliced
- 2 tablespoons garlic, sliced
- ½ cup tomato, diced
- ½ cup carrots, sliced
- 2 tablespoons tomato paste
- Salt and pepper to taste
- 1 ½ teaspoons ground cumin
- 2 ½ cups red or yellow lentils
- 9 cups water

Instructions:

1. Pour the oil into a pot over medium heat.

2. Add the onion, garlic, tomato and carrots.

3. Cook for 5 minutes, stirring occasionally.

4. Stir in the tomato paste.

5. Season with the salt, pepper and cumin.

6. Cook while stirring frequently for 2 minutes.

7. Add the lentils to the pot.

8. Increase heat and bring to a boil.

9. Reduce heat and simmer for 25 minutes. Let the mixture cool.

10. Once cool enough to handle, transfer to a blender.

11. Blend until smooth.

12. Reheat before serving.

Nutrients per Serving:

- Calories 245
- Fat 3.2 g
- Saturated fat 0.4 g
- Carbohydrates 41.1 g
- Fiber 7.3 g
- Protein 14.9 g
- Cholesterol 13 mg
- Sugars 1 g
- Sodium 487 mg
- Potassium 513 mg

Moroccan Chicken, Couscous Veggies

Overloaded with flavors and colors, this Moroccan dish is a mix of chicken, couscous, chickpeas, butternut squash, and apricots. Not only that, but it's also packed with protein, fiber, and vitamins.

Serving Size: 8

Preparation Cooking Time: 4 hours and 30 minutes

Ingredients:

- ½ teaspoon ground ginger
- ½ teaspoon ground cumin
- ¼ teaspoon cayenne pepper
- ¼ teaspoon ground cinnamon
- Salt and pepper to taste
- 8 chicken thighs
- 1 tablespoon olive oil
- 4 oz. yellow onions, chopped
- 1 cup chicken stock
- 16 oz. butternut squash, chopped
- 15 oz. chickpeas, rinsed and drained
- 3 oz. dried apricots, sliced in half
- 1 ¾ whole-wheat couscous, cooked without oil and salt
- Cilantro, chopped
- ¼ cup almonds, toasted and sliced

Instructions:

1. Combine the ginger, cumin, cayenne, cinnamon, salt and pepper in a bowl.

2. Rub the chicken with the mixture.

3. Pour the oil into a pan over medium high heat.

4. Cook the chicken for 3 to 4 minutes per side.

5. Transfer the chicken to a slow cooker.

6. Cook the onions in the pan for 4 minutes.

7. Sprinkle the onions on top of the chicken.

8. Pour in the chicken stock.

9. Add the squash, chickpeas and dried apricots.

10. Season with the salt.

11. Cover the pot.

12. Cook on low for 4 hours.

13. Transfer the couscous in serving bowls.

14. Add the chicken mixture on top.

15. Garnish with the cilantro and almonds before serving.

Nutrients per Serving:

- Calories 496

- Fat 15 g

- Saturated fat 3 g

- Carbohydrates 49 g

- Fiber 7 g

- Protein 43 g

- Cholesterol 29 mg

- Sugars 7 g

- Sodium 453 mg

- Potassium 445 mg

Koshari

Koshari is vegetarian comfort food that originated in Cairo in the 1800s. Most kosharis are topped with crispy onions, vinegar, and tomato sauce.

Serving Size: 8

Preparation Cooking Time: 45 minutes

Ingredients:

Koshari

- 1 tablespoon sunflower oil
- 1 ⅓ cups brown basmati rice
- Salt and pepper to taste
- 2 teaspoons ground cumin
- 2 ⅔ cups water
- 4 oz. spaghetti, cooked according to the directions in the package
- 15 oz. brown lentils, rinsed and drained
- 15 oz. chickpeas, rinsed and drained

Shatta

- ½ cup onion, chopped
- 2 cloves garlic, sliced
- 1 tablespoon tomato paste
- 2 cups canned diced tomatoes
- 6 tablespoons ground cumin
- 1 tablespoon white vinegar
- 1 ⅓ cups water
- Salt and pepper to taste
- 1 teaspoon cayenne pepper
- 1 tablespoon red-wine vinegar

Crispy Onions

- 1 ½ cups sunflower oil

- 1 cup white onion, sliced

- 2 tablespoons cornstarch

- Salt to taste

Dakka

- 1 teaspoon garlic, minced

- 3 tablespoons white vinegar

- ¾ cup water

- ½ teaspoon ground cumin

- Salt to taste

Instructions:

1. First, prepare the koshari by adding the oil into a pan over medium heat.

2. Cook the rice while stirring for 1 minute.

3. Add the salt, pepper and cumin.

4. Cook for 1 minute.

5. Pour in the water.

6. Increase heat and bring to a boil.

7. Reduce heat and then simmer for 35 minutes.

8. Remove from the stove.

9. Let sit for 5 minutes.

10. Next, prepare the shatta by combining the onion, garlic, tomato paste, diced tomatoes, cumin, vinegar, water, salt and pepper in a pan over medium high heat.

11. Bring to a boil.

12. Reduce heat and then simmer for 20 minutes, stirring occasionally.

13. Remove from the stove.

14. Stir in the cayenne and red wine vinegar.

15. Next, prepare the fried onions by adding the oil to a pan over medium heat.

16. Coat the onion with the cornstarch.

17. Cook the onion in hot oil for 6 minutes.

18. Season with the salt.

19. Finally, prepare the dakka by combining all the dakka ingredients in a blender.

20. Pulse until smooth.

21. Transfer the mixture to a bowl.

22. Transfer the shatta to the blender.

23. Pulse until smooth.

24. Stir the lentils and cooked spaghetti into the rice.

25. Top with the chickpeas, crispy onions, dakka and shatta.

Nutrients per Serving:

- Calories 350

- Fat 11.6 g

- Saturated fat 1 g

- Carbohydrates 53.2 g

- Fiber 10 g

- Protein 11.1 g

- Cholesterol 13 mg

- Sugars 4 g

- Sodium 674 mg

- Potassium 308 mg

Moroccan Chicken Stew

What makes this Moroccan chicken stew incredible? It is the perfect blending of chicken, chickpeas, sweet potatoes, ginger, and spices.

Serving Size: 8

Preparation Cooking Time: 5 hours and 30 minutes

Ingredients:

- 1 teaspoon ground cumin
- ½ teaspoon ground coriander
- ¼ teaspoon cayenne pepper
- ½ teaspoon ground cinnamon
- 8 chicken thighs, fat trimmed
- 2 tablespoons olive oil
- 1 onion, sliced
- 2 teaspoons ginger, minced
- 1 ½ cups chicken stock (unsalted)
- 1 sweet potato, chopped
- 15 oz. chickpeas, rinsed and drained
- 28 oz. canned tomatoes, chopped
- Salt to taste
- ¼ cup raisins
- 1 teaspoon lemon zest
- ¼ cup cilantro, chopped

Instructions:

1. Combine the cumin, coriander, cayenne pepper and cinnamon in a bowl.

2. Season the chicken with this mixture.

3. Pour the olive oil into a pan over medium high heat.

4. Cook the chicken for 3 minutes per side.

5. Transfer to a slow cooker.

6. Add the ginger and onion to the pan.

7. Cook for 3 minutes.

8. Pour the stock into the pan.

9. Cook for 1 minute

10. Scrape the browned bits on the bottom of the pan.

11. Add the onion mixture, sweet potato, chickpeas, canned tomatoes, salt and raisins to the pot.

12. Cover the pot.

13. Cook on low for 5 hours.

14. Transfer the chicken to a cutting board.

15. Slice into smaller pieces.

16. Put the chicken back to the pan.

17. Add the lemon zest.

18. Top with the cilantro before serving.

Nutrients per Serving:

- Calories 302

- Fat 9 g

- Saturated fat 2 g

- Carbohydrates 23 g

- Fiber 4 g

- Protein 31 g

- Cholesterol 11 mg

- Sugars 8 g

- Sodium 608 mg

- Potassium 556 mg

Tunisian Roasted Veggies

Make your roasted vegetables spicier and more appetizing by seasoning them with harissa paste. It's also a good idea to add sliced hard-boiled eggs, canned tuna flakes, and Kalamata olives to add more depth to the dish.

Serving Size: 6

Preparation Cooking Time: 1 hour and 5 minutes

Ingredients:

- 3 cups cauliflower florets
- 2 red bell peppers, sliced
- 2 cups cherry tomatoes, sliced
- 3 tablespoons olive oil
- 2 tablespoons sherry vinegar
- 1 clove garlic, crushed and minced
- 1 teaspoon caraway seeds, crushed
- Salt and pepper to taste
- 2 teaspoons harissa paste
- 12 oz. canned tuna flakes
- ¼ cup Kalamata olives, pitted and sliced in half
- 3 hard-boiled eggs, sliced in half

Instructions:

1. Preheat your oven to 400 degrees F.

2. Spray your baking pan with oil.

3. Arrange the cauliflower in the pan.

4. Roast in the oven for 10 minutes.

5. Stir in the bell peppers and tomatoes.

6. Roast for another 20 minutes.

7. Make the vinaigrette by mixing the olive oil, vinegar, garlic, caraway seeds, salt, pepper and harissa paste in a bowl.

8. Take 2 tablespoons of the vinaigrette and add to a bowl.

9. Stir in the tuna.

10. Drizzle the remaining vinaigrette over the roasted veggies.

11. Coat evenly and roast for another 15 minutes.

12. Serve the roasted veggies with the tuna, olives and eggs.

Nutrients per Serving:

- Calories 189
- Fat 11.4 g
- Saturated fat 1.8 g
- Carbohydrates 8.7 g
- Fiber 3.1 g
- Protein 13.4 g
- Cholesterol 112 mg
- Sugars 5 g
- Sodium 364 mg
- Potassium 517 mg

Shrimp Peanut Soup

This creamy peanut soup is made by pureeing peanut butter along with tomatoes and squash and topping it with tangy shrimp and crunchy carrot strips.

Serving Size: 8

Preparation Cooking Time: 2 hours

Ingredients:

- Cooking spray
- 1 lb. shrimp, peeled and deveined
- 2 ½ lb. butternut squash, sliced in half
- ½ teaspoon ground coriander
- 2 teaspoons ground cumin
- ¼ teaspoon ground turmeric
- ¼ teaspoon ground cinnamon
- Salt and pepper to taste
- 2 teaspoons toasted sesame oil
- 1 onion, chopped
- 3 cloves garlic, crushed and minced
- 1 red bell pepper, chopped
- 1 tablespoon freshly grated ginger
- 2 teaspoons jalapeño chili pepper, chopped
- ¾ cup creamy peanut butter
- 2 tablespoons green curry paste
- 1 teaspoon low-sodium soy sauce
- 3 cups reduced-sodium vegetable broth
- 30 oz. canned diced tomatoes
- 2 cups carrots, sliced into thin strips and steamed

Instructions:

1. Preheat your oven to 450 degrees F.

2. Line your baking pan with foil.

3. Spray it with oil.

4. Add the squash to the baking pan.

5. Roast for 45 minutes.

6. Scrape the flesh and mash with a fork.

7. In a bowl, mix the coriander, cumin, turmeric, cinnamon, salt and pepper.

8. Season the shrimp with 2 teaspoons of this mixture.

9. Place the shrimp in another bowl.

10. Cover the bowl with the shrimp and refrigerate.

11. Pour the sesame oil into a pot over medium heat.

12. Add the onion, garlic, bell pepper, ginger and chili pepper.

13. Cook for 5 minutes.

14. Stir in the remaining spice blend along with the peanut butter, curry paste, soy sauce, vegetable broth and tomatoes.

15. Bring to a boil.

16. Reduce heat and simmer for 30 minutes.

17. Spray your pan with oil.

18. Put it over medium heat.

19. Cook the shrimp for 5 minutes.

20. Top the soup with the shrimp and carrot strips.

Nutrients per Serving:

- Calories 276

- Fat 13.8 g

- Saturated fat 2.8 g

- Carbohydrates 23.9 g

- Fiber 7.1 g

- Protein 18.2 g

- Cholesterol 79 mg

- Sugars 11 g

- Sodium 584 mg

- Potassium 649 mg

Chicken Snow Peas

Season your chicken and snow peas with harissa sauce in this quick and easy dinner recipe that only takes 20 minutes to complete.

Serving Size: 4

Preparation Cooking Time: 25 minutes

Ingredients:

- 1 lb. chicken breast fillet, sliced into cubes
- 2 cloves garlic, crushed and minced
- 2 teaspoons harissa paste
- 1 tablespoon olive oil
- ½ cup low-sodium chicken stock
- 12 oz. snow peas, trimmed
- 15 oz. chickpeas, rinsed and drained
- 2 cups cherry tomatoes, sliced in half
- Salt to taste
- ¼ cup Kalamata olives, pitted and sliced in half
- ¼ cup fresh parsley leaves, chopped
- 1 teaspoon lemon zest
- 1 tablespoon lemon juice
- ¼ cup nonfat Greek yogurt (plain)

Instructions:

1. In a bowl, mix the chicken, garlic and harissa paste.

2. Pour the oil into a pan over medium heat.

3. Cook the chicken for 3 to 4 minutes per side.

4. Transfer to a plate.

5. In the same pan, add the chicken stock, snow peas, chickpeas, cherry tomatoes and salt.

6. Bring to a boil.

7. Reduce heat and simmer for 5 minutes.

8. Put the chicken back to the pan.

9. Add the olives, parsley, lemon zest and lemon juice to the pan.

10. Remove from heat.

11. Transfer the chicken mixture into serving bowls.

12. Top with the yogurt.

Nutrients per Serving:

- Calories 323
- Fat 10 g
- Saturated fat 1.2 g
- Carbohydrates 23 g
- Fiber 6.6 g
- Protein 34.5 g
- Cholesterol 83 mg
- Sugars 7 g
- Sodium 502 mg
- Potassium 827 mg

Moroccan Roasted Fish Veggies

Roast your fish and veggies seasoned with ras el hanout. Top these with the popular Moroccan sauce called chermoula. Chermoula is made by mixing garlic, paprika, herbs, and lemon juice.

Serving Size: 4

Preparation Cooking Time: 50 minutes

Ingredients:

- 2 cups green bell pepper, sliced

- 1 jalapeño pepper, sliced into thin rings

- 2 tomatoes, sliced thinly

- 1 potato, sliced into thin strips

- 3 tablespoons olive oil, divided

- 1 teaspoon ras el hanout spice blend

- 2 tablespoons lemon juice

- 2 teaspoons lemon zest

- 3 cloves garlic, crushed and minced

- 2 tablespoons parsley, chopped

- 1 teaspoon paprika

- Salt to taste

- 2 tablespoons fresh cilantro, chopped

- 4 cod fillets

Instructions:

1. Preheat your oven to 425 degrees F.

2. Toss the potato, green bell pepper, jalapeño pepper, tomatoes, and potato in 1 tablespoon oil.

3. Season with the ras el hanout.

4. Transfer the vegetable mixture to a baking pan.

5. Roast for 20 minutes, stirring halfway through.

6. Combine the lemon juice, lemon zest, garlic, parsley, paprika, cilantro, salt and remaining oil in a bowl.

7. Add the fish on top of the vegetables.

8. Drizzle with the lemon garlic mixture.

9. Roast in the oven for 15 minutes.

Nutrients per Serving:

- Calories 284
- Fat 11.6 g
- Saturated fat 1.7 g
- Carbohydrates 28.1 g
- Fiber 4.8 g
- Protein 19.1 g
- Cholesterol 45 mg
- Sugars 5 g
- Sodium 610 mg
- Potassium 1058 mg

Moroccan Chicken Legs

The trick to this dish is to slow grill the chicken to infuse it with the flavors of the herbs and spices. Serve with saffron rice or couscous.

Serving Size: 4

Preparation Cooking Time: 5 hours and 10 minutes

Ingredients:

- 1 tablespoon olive oil
- ½ teaspoon ground coriander
- 1 teaspoon ground cumin
- 1 teaspoon paprika
- ¼ teaspoon red pepper flakes
- Salt to taste
- 1 tablespoon freshly grated ginger
- ½ cup freshly squeezed orange juice
- 2 lb. chicken legs, skin removed
- 2 teaspoons freshly squeezed orange juice
- 2 tablespoons honey
- 2 teaspoons orange zest

Instructions:

1. In a bowl, mix the olive oil, cumin, paprika, ginger, red pepper flakes, coriander, salt and ½ cup orange juice.

2. Add the chicken to this bowl.

3. Turn to coat evenly.

4. Cover the bowl with foil.

5. Refrigerate for 4 hours.

6. In another bowl, combine 2 teaspoons orange juice with the honey and orange zest.

7. Add the chicken to a grill rack and place over the drip pan.

8. Cover and cook for 60 minutes, brush with the orange honey mixture.

Nutrients per Serving:

- Calories 251
- Fat 9.1 g
- Saturated fat 2.3 g
- Carbohydrates 11.3 g
- Fiber 0.5 g
- Protein 29.8 g
- Cholesterol 92 mg
- Sugars 10 g
- Sodium 121 mg
- Potassium 317 mg

Green Shakshuka

Shakshuka is a well-known breakfast dish in Israel and Northern Africa. It is made by poaching eggs in herbed tomato sauce. In this version, we add tomatillos and spinach to the dish.

Serving Size: 4

Preparation Cooking Time: 30 minutes

Ingredients:

- 2 tablespoons olive oil

- 1 cup scallions, chopped

- 2 cloves garlic, chopped

- 1 serrano pepper, chopped

- 1 teaspoon ground cumin

- 8 oz. green tomatoes, chopped

- 8 cups spinach

- ¼ cup water

- ¼ cup fresh cilantro, chopped

- ½ cup parsley, chopped

- Salt to taste

- ¼ cup fresh mint leaves, chopped

- 4 eggs

- ¼ cup feta cheese, crumbled

- Harissa paste

- Freshly cracked black pepper

Instructions:

1. Add the oil into a pan over medium heat.

2. Cook the scallions for 2 minutes.

3. Stir in the garlic and season with the cumin and pepper.

4. Cook for 30 seconds.

5. Add the green tomatoes and cook for 5 minutes.

6. Stir in the spinach.

7. Pour in the water.

8. Cook for 1 minute.

9. Add the cilantro, parsley, salt and mint. Stir.

10. Crack the eggs on top.

11. Cover the pan and cook for 3 minutes.

12. Sprinkle with the feta.

13. Cook for 2 minutes.

14. Sprinkle the harissa and pepper on top.

Nutrients per Serving:

- Calories 210

- Fat 14.8 g

- Saturated fat 4.1 g

- Carbohydrates 9.9 g

- Fiber 4 g

- Protein 11 g

- Cholesterol 194 mg

- Sugars 4 g

- Sodium 362 mg

- Potassium 718 mg

Pot Roast Veggies

Pot roast with veggies is a popular dish almost anywhere in the world. But what makes this particular recipe unique is that it is infused with Moroccan flavors. Expect it to be more pungent, more flavorful, and more exciting.

Serving Size: 6

Preparation Cooking Time: 5 hours and 30 minutes

Ingredients:

- 1 teaspoon ground cumin
- 2 teaspoons pumpkin pie spice
- Salt and pepper to taste
- 2 ½ lb. beef chuck roast, fat trimmed
- 1 tablespoon olive oil
- 1 lb. carrots, sliced
- 3 cups parsnips, sliced
- 2 onions, sliced into wedges
- 3 tablespoons tapioca, crushed
- 1 cup low-sodium beef broth
- ½ teaspoon mustard
- 2 tablespoons tomato paste
- 2 sweet peppers, sliced
- Fresh cilantro, chopped

Instructions:

1. In a bowl, mix the cumin, pumpkin pie spice, salt and pepper.

2. Season the beef with this mixture.

3. In a pan over medium heat, cook the beef until brown on all sides.

4. Add the parsnips and carrots to your slow cooker along with your beef.

5. Sprinkle the onions on top.

6. In another bowl, combine the tapioca, beef broth, mustard and tomato paste.

7. Season with the salt and pepper.

8. Pour this mixture into the pot.

9. Cover the pot.

10. Cook on low for 4 hours and 30 minutes.

11. Stir in the peppers.

12. Cook on high for 30 minutes.

13. Transfer the beef and veggies to a plate.

14. Skim the fat.

15. Pour the cooking liquid over the beef and veggies.

16. Garnish with the cilantro.

Nutrients per Serving:

- Calories 414
- Fat 8.8 g
- Saturated fat 3.1 g
- Carbohydrates 37.4 g
- Fiber 8.6 g
- Protein 45.6 g
- Cholesterol 123 mg
- Sugars 14 g
- Sodium 473 mg
- Potassium 1457 mg

Egg Tomato in a Skillet

This favorite North African comfort food is served not only during breakfast but can also be eaten during lunch or dinner.

Serving Size: 4

Preparation Cooking Time: 40 minutes

Ingredients:

- 2 tablespoons olive oil
- ½ cup onion, chopped
- 1 teaspoon smoked paprika
- 2 tablespoons tomato paste
- 2 cups red sweet peppers, chopped
- 2 teaspoons red pepper flakes
- 3 cups tomatoes, chopped
- Salt to taste
- 1 teaspoon ground cumin
- 4 eggs
- ½ cup nonfat Greek yogurt
- Fresh parsley, chopped
- 2 pita breads (preferably whole-wheat)

Instructions:

1. Pour the oil into a pan over medium heat.

2. Cook the onion, paprika, tomato paste, peppers and red pepper flakes for 7 minutes.

3. Add the tomatoes, salt and cumin.

4. Bring to a boil.

5. Reduce heat and simmer for 10 minutes.

6. Break the eggs on top of the tomato sauce.

7. Simmer for 4 minutes.

8. Spread the yogurt and sprinkle the parsley on top.

Nutrients per Serving:

- Calories 303

- Fat 13 g

- Saturated fat 3 g

- Carbohydrates 33 g

- Fiber 6 g

- Protein 15 g

- Cholesterol 189 mg

- Sugars 11 g

- Sodium 410 mg

- Potassium 556 mg

Moroccan Lamb Chops

Sprinkle your lamb chops with the African spice blend ras el hanout to transform them into something unforgettable. Serve with a fresh green salad, salsa, or steamed potatoes.

Serving Size: 4

Preparation Cooking Time: 20 minutes

Ingredients:

- ¼ cup olives, chopped
- 1 cup tomatoes, chopped
- ¼ cup parsley, chopped
- 2 tablespoons olive oil, divided
- Pepper to taste
- 8 lamb chops
- 1 tablespoon ras el hanout

Instructions:

1. Preheat your grill.

2. In a bowl, mix the olives, tomatoes, parsley and 1 tablespoon oil.

3. Season with the pepper.

4. Brush the lamb chops with the remaining oil.

5. Sprinkle both sides with the ras el hanout.

6. Grill for 2 minutes per side.

7. Serve with the olive relish.

Nutrients per Serving:

- Calories 427
- Fat 27.4 g
- Saturated fat 7.7 g
- Carbohydrates 3.2 g
- Fiber 1.4 g
- Protein 37.2 g
- Cholesterol 125 mg
- Sugars 1 g
- Sodium 296 mg
- Potassium 128 mg

Chili Chicken Thighs

Season your chicken thighs with a mix of ginger, cumin, cinnamon, and chili powder. Serve with steamed veggies and couscous.

Serving Size: 4

Preparation Cooking Time: 1 hour

Ingredients:

- 2 tablespoons flour
- ½ teaspoon ground cumin
- 1 teaspoon chili powder
- ¼ teaspoon ground cinnamon
- ½ teaspoon ground ginger
- 4 chicken thighs
- 2 teaspoons cooking oil

Instructions:

1. Preheat your oven to 375 degrees F.

2. In a bowl, mix the flour, cumin, chili powder, cinnamon and ginger.

3. Coat the chicken with this mixture.

4. Pour the oil into a pan over medium heat.

5. Cook the chicken thighs for 5 minutes.

6. Place the pan inside the oven.

7. Bake for 40 minutes.

Nutrients per Serving:

- Calories 138

- Fat 5.8 g

- Saturated fat 1 g

- Carbohydrates 3.7 g

- Fiber 0.5 g

- Protein 16.9 g

- Cholesterol 81 mg

- Sugars 3 g

- Sodium 72 mg

- Potassium 192 mg

Injera

Injera refers to Ethiopian flatbread. Stuff with your favorite fillings—beef, veggies and herbs, or eat it plain.

Serving Size: 12

Preparation Cooking Time: 3 days

Ingredients:

- 1 cup self-rising flour
- 2 cups teff flour
- 1 cup corn flour
- 1 cup barley flour
- 1 teaspoon active dry yeast
- 6 cups lukewarm water

Instructions:

1. Combine the four types of flour and dry yeast in a bowl.

2. Gradually add water and mix until smooth.

3. Let stand at room temperature for 3 days.

4. Remove the water on the surface and set aside.

5. Mix the remaining batter.

6. Cover and let stand at room temperature for another 1 hour.

7. Put a pan over medium heat.

8. Add ½ cup batter into the pan.

9. Create a thin layer by swirling the batter around.

10. When you see holes forming on the surface, cover the pan.

11. Cook for 45 seconds.

12. Repeat the steps for the remaining batter.

Nutrients per Serving:

- Calories 216

- Fat 1.7 g

- Saturated fat 0.1 g

- Carbohydrates 43.9 g

- Fiber 5.7 g

- Protein 6.5 g

- Cholesterol 17 mg

- Sugars 10 g

- Sodium 132 mg

- Potassium 86 mg

Fish Sweet Potato Bowl

Here's a simple bowl dinner recipe that only takes 5 ingredients and 45 minutes to prepare.

Serving Size: 2

Preparation Cooking Time: 45 minutes

Ingredients:

- Cooking spray
- 2 tablespoons olive oil
- 1 tablespoon harissa
- Salt to taste
- 1 sweet potato, sliced into cubes
- 1 salmon fillet, sliced
- 1 cup cooked farro
- 2 cups baby spinach

Instructions:

1. Preheat your oven to 425 degrees F.

2. Spray your baking pan with oil.

3. In a bowl, mix the harissa, olive oil and salt.

4. Coat the sweet potato in this mixture.

5. Place these on a baking pan.

6. Roast for 20 minutes.

7. Brush the remaining harissa mixture on both sides of the fish.

8. Add the salmon to the baking pan.

9. Roast for 8 to 10 minutes.

10. Combine the farro and spinach, and transfer to a serving bowl.

11. Top with the roasted salmon and sweet potatoes.

Nutrients per Serving:

- Calories 662

- Fat 28.9 g

- Saturated fat 4.7 g

- Carbohydrates 61.1 g

- Fiber 8.9 g

- Protein 35.5 g

- Cholesterol 73 mg

- Sugars 9 g

- Sodium 986 mg

- Potassium 655 mg

Fossolia

Season your green beans with ginger, garlic, rosemary, and makulaya alicha spice blend to create an incredible side dish.

Serving Size: 4

Preparation Cooking Time: 1 hour

Ingredients:

- 1 teaspoon makulaya alicha spice blend

- 4 tablespoons olive oil, divided

- ¼ teaspoon ground cumin

- 1 bowl hot water

- 1 tomato

- 1 cup yellow onion, sliced

- ¼ cup ginger, minced

- 1 lb. green beans, trimmed and sliced in half

- 2 ½ tablespoons garlic, minced

- 2 tablespoons water

- Salt to taste

- 1 sprig fresh rosemary

Instructions:

1. Soak the green beans in a bowl of hot water for 10 minutes.

2. Drain the water.

3. Pat the beans dry using paper towels.

4. Place your pan over medium high heat.

5. Cook the tomato for 10 minutes, stirring frequently.

6. Transfer the tomato to a bowl and let cool.

7. Puree in a blender.

8. Pour half of the olive oil to a pan over medium heat.

9. Cook the green beans for 5 minutes.

10. Transfer to a plate.

11. Pour the remaining oil.

12. Cook the onion, garlic and ginger for 3 minutes.

13. Add the water to the pan.

14. Cook for another 4 minutes.

15. Stir in the tomato puree and the rest of the ingredients.

16. Cook for 3 minutes.

Nutrients per Serving:

- Calories 199

- Fat 14.5 g

- Saturated fat 2.1 g

- Carbohydrates 16.4 g

- Fiber 4.5 g

- Protein 3.3 g

- Cholesterol 15 mg

- Sugars 6 g

- Sodium 153 mg

- Potassium 440 mg

Kinche

Kinche refers to grain porridge that is often eating during breakfast. But you can also top it with spiced collards or lentils and serve it during lunch or dinner.

Serving Size: 8

Preparation Cooking Time: 20 minutes

Ingredients:

- 1 ¼ cups bulgur, rinsed and drained
- 2 cups water
- ¼ cup olive oil
- Salt to taste

Instructions:

1. Add the bulgur and water in a saucepan.

2. Bring to a boil.

3. Reduce heat.

4. Cover the pan.

5. Simmer for 10 minutes.

6. Remove from the stove.

7. Let sit for 5 minutes without removing the cover.

8. Stir in the olive oil, and season with the salt before serving.

Nutrients per Serving:

- Calories 139

- Fat 7.4 g

- Saturated fat 4.3 g

- Carbohydrates 16.6 g

- Fiber 2.7 g

- Protein 2.9 g

- Cholesterol 11 mg

- Sugars 3 g

- Sodium 75 mg

- Potassium 90 mg

Doro Alicha

Doro Alicha is a chicken stew made with spiced butter sauce and onions. It is similar to the popular chicken stew in Ethiopia, but instead of using hot pepper spices, this one is seasoned with garlic, ginger, and turmeric.

Serving Size: 4

Preparation Cooking Time: 1 hour and 45 minutes

Ingredients:

- 4 chicken legs, trimmed and skinned

- Salt to taste

- 2 tablespoons freshly squeezed lemon juice

- 3 cups onion, minced

- 5 cups water, divided

- ¼ cup clarified butter

- ¼ cup ginger, minced

- 2 ½ tablespoons garlic, minced

- 1 teaspoon ground turmeric

- ½ teaspoon dried basil

- ½ teaspoon dried thyme

- ½ teaspoon cardamom

- ½ teaspoon cinnamon

- Pepper to taste

- 1 cup dry white wine

- 2 hard-boiled eggs

Instructions:

1. Add the chicken to a dish.

2. Season it with the salt and drizzle with the lemon juice.

3. Add the onions to a pot over medium heat.

4. Cook for 5 minutes.

5. Pour 1/4 cup water into the pot.

6. Cook for 20 minutes.

7. Stir in the butter and ginger.

8. Reduce heat and cook while stirring for 10 minutes.

9. Increase heat and add the garlic and herbs.

10. Cook for 1 minute.

11. Pour in the wine.

12. Cook for 5 minutes.

13. Add the chicken.

14. Add more water to cover the chicken.

15. Increase heat. Bring to a boil.

16. Reduce heat and simmer for 30 minutes.

17. Transfer the chicken to a bowl.

18. Continue boiling the sauce until reduced by half.

19. Add the eggs to the sauce.

20. Slice the eggs in half.

21. Add the eggs and sauce to the bowl with the chicken and serve.

Nutrients per Serving:

- Calories 483

- Fat 26.9 g

- Saturated fat 12.1 g

- Carbohydrates 19.6 g

- Fiber 2.6 g

- Protein 35.9 g

- Cholesterol 278 mg

- Sugars 5 g

- Sodium 454 mg

- Potassium 634 mg

Spaghetti Squash

In this spaghetti squash recipe, the squash strands are seasoned with a spice blend called dukka. It is made by mixing crushed cumin seeds, coriander seeds, and sesame seeds.

Serving Size: 6

Preparation Cooking Time: 1 hour

Ingredients:

- 3 ½ lb. spaghetti squash, sliced in half and seeds removed
- 3 tablespoons olive oil, divided
- Salt and pepper to taste
- 4 cloves garlic
- ½ cup water
- ½ cup dukkah
- 2 tablespoons fresh cilantro leaves, chopped

Instructions:

1. Preheat your oven to 425 degrees F.

2. Coat the squash halves with 1 tablespoon olive oil.

3. Season with the salt and pepper.

4. Place in a baking pan with the cut-side down.

5. Place the garlic under the squash halves.

6. Roast in the oven for 30 minutes.

7. Turn the squash upside down.

8. Rub the roasted garlic on the cut-side

9. Let cool.

10. Scrape the flesh into strands.

11. Season with the dukkah and drizzle with the remaining oil.

12. Garnish with the fresh cilantro.

Nutrients per Serving:

- Calories 197

- Fat 14.1 g

- Saturated fat 1.8 g

- Carbohydrates 17.4 g

- Fiber 4.4 g

- Protein 3.8 g

- Cholesterol 15 mg

- Sugars 6 g

- Sodium 139 mg

- Potassium 362 mg

Lemon Lamb Tagine

Here's another lamb tagine that you'll have fun preparing. This one is served with yogurt seasoned with paprika and lemon salsa verde.

Serving Size: 8

Preparation Cooking Time: 4 hours

Ingredients:

Tagine

- 3 lb. lamb shoulder, trimmed and sliced into cubes
- 4 teaspoons ras el hanout
- Salt to taste
- 1 onion, chopped
- 4 tablespoons garlic, chopped and divided
- 3 tablespoons ginger, grated and divided
- 1 lb. turnips, sliced
- 1 lb. carrots, sliced into cubes
- ¼ cup lemon rind, chopped
- ½ teaspoon red pepper flakes

Toppings

- 1 cup nonfat Green yogurt
- 4 tablespoons freshly squeezed lemon juice, divided
- Salt to taste
- ½ teaspoon smoked paprika
- 2 tablespoons olive oil
- 1 cup parsley, chopped
- ¼ cup lemon rind, chopped
- 1 cup fresh mint leaves, chopped
- Pistachios, chopped

Instructions:

1. Season the lamb cubes with the salt and ras el hanout.

2. Put the lamb cubes in a slow cooker.

3. Add the onion, 3 tablespoons garlic, 2 tablespoons ginger, turnips, carrots, and lemon rind to the slow cooker.

4. Cover the pot.

5. Cook on high for 3 hours.

6. Stir in the remaining ginger and garlic along with the red pepper flakes.

7. Cover the pot and cook for another 10 minutes.

8. In a bowl, mix the yogurt, half of the lemon juice, salt and paprika.

9. In another bowl, mix the olive oil, remaining lemon juice, parsley, lemon rind and mint leaves.

10. Top the lamb tagine with the yogurt mixture and herb mixture.

11. Sprinkle the pistachios on top.

Nutrients per Serving:

- Calories 397

- Fat 21.1 g

- Saturated fat 7 g

- Carbohydrates 16.5 g

- Fiber 4.2 g

- Protein 35.4 g

- Cholesterol 112 mg

- Sugars 7 g

- Sodium 557 mg

- Potassium 692 mg

Roasted Carrots

Have you tried making hasselback potatoes? In this version, we use carrots instead of potatoes, and season it with strong herbs and spices for an unforgettable meal that everyone will love.

Serving Size: 4

Preparation Cooking Time: 45 minutes

Ingredients:

- Cooking spray
- 4 carrots, trimmed
- 2 cloves garlic, sliced thinly
- 2 tablespoons olive oil, divided
- 2 tablespoons freshly squeezed lemon juice
- Salt and pepper to taste
- 1 teaspoon ground cumin
- 1 teaspoon ground coriander
- 1 teaspoon paprika
- 1 tablespoon Kalamata olives, chopped
- 2 tablespoons parsley, chopped

Instructions:

1. Preheat your oven to 400 degrees F.

2. Spray your baking pan with oil.

3. Make several crosswise slits along the carrots but do not slice all the way through.

4. Insert garlic slices in the slits.

5. Add the carrots to the baking pan.

6. Pour 1 tablespoon oil over the carrots.

7. Bake for 35 minutes.

8. In a bowl, mix the lemon juice, remaining oil, salt, pepper, cumin, coriander and paprika.

9. Place the carrots on a serving plate.

10. Drizzle the lemon mixture on top of the carrots.

11. Sprinkle the olives and parsley on top.

Nutrients per Serving:

- Calories 108

- Fat 8.4 g

- Saturated fat 1.1 g

- Carbohydrates 8.1 g

- Fiber 2.4 g

- Protein 1 g

- Cholesterol 13 mg

- Sugars 3 g

- Sodium 173 mg

- Potassium 234 mg

Acorn Stuffed with Chickpeas

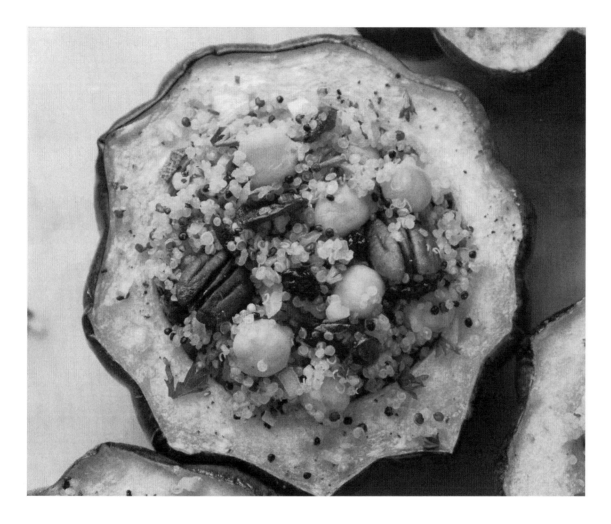

Here's a healthy and delicious vegetarian side dish that's well-loved in many parts of Africa—acorn squash sliced in half and stuffed with spiced chickpeas.

Serving Size: 8

Preparation Cooking Time: 1 hour and 15 minutes

Ingredients:

- 4 acorn squash, sliced in half and seeded

- 3 tablespoons vegetable oil, divided

- Salt to taste

- 1 cinnamon stick, broken

- 2 tablespoons coriander seeds

- 1 teaspoon cumin seeds

- ½ teaspoon cayenne pepper

- ¼ teaspoon ground turmeric

- 1 teaspoon smoked paprika

- 1 cup onion, chopped

- 4 cloves garlic, chopped

- 3 cups butternut squash, sliced into cubes

- 15 oz. canned diced tomatoes

- 1 ¼ cups water

- 30 oz. chickpeas, rinsed and drained

- ¼ cup fresh cilantro, chopped

Instructions:

1. Preheat your oven to 375 degrees F.

2. Spray your baking pan with oil.

3. Drizzle the squash halves with 1 tablespoon oil.

4. Season with the salt.

5. Place in the baking pan, cut-side down.

6. Bake in the oven for 45 minutes.

7. Add the cumin seeds, coriander and cinnamon stick in a spice grinder and process to grind.

8. Transfer the spice blend to a bowl.

9. Stir in the cayenne, turmeric, paprika and salt.

10. Pour 2 tablespoons oil into a pot over medium heat.

11. Cook the onion and garlic for 5 minutes.

12. Add the spice mixture and squash cubes.

13. Cook for 30 seconds, stirring frequently.

14. Stir in the tomatoes with juice, water and chickpeas.

15. Bring to a boil.

16. Reduce heat and simmer for 10 minutes.

17. Stir in the fresh cilantro.

18. Stuff the squash halves with the chickpea mixture and serve.

Nutrients per Serving:

- Calories 267

- Fat 7.1 g

- Saturated fat 0.6 g

- Carbohydrates 49.2 g

- Fiber 9.8 g

- Protein 7.1 g

- Cholesterol 13 mg

- Sugars 8 g

- Sodium 442 mg

- Potassium 1146 mg

Spicy Carrots

Spice up your carrot slices with North African favorites: cumin, paprika, and coriander.

Serving Size: 6

Preparation Cooking Time: 20 minutes

Ingredients:

- 1 tablespoon olive oil
- 4 cloves garlic, crushed and minced
- 1 teaspoon ground cumin
- 1 teaspoon ground coriander
- 2 teaspoons paprika
- 4 carrots, sliced
- Salt to taste
- 3 tablespoons freshly squeezed lemon juice
- 1 cup water
- ¼ cup fresh parsley, chopped

Instructions:

1. Pour the oil into a pan over medium heat.

2. Add the garlic.

3. Season with the cumin, coriander and paprika.

4. Cook for 20 seconds, stirring frequently.

5. Stir in the carrots, salt, lemon juice and water.

6. Bring to a simmer.

7. Reduce heat and cover.

8. Cook for 7 minutes.

9. Uncover the pan.

10. Cook for 4 minutes.

11. Add the parsley and serve.

Nutrients per Serving:

- Calories 51
- Fat 2.7 g
- Saturated fat 0.4 g
- Carbohydrates 6.7 g
- Fiber 2.3 g
- Protein 0.8 g
- Cholesterol 13 mg
- Sugars 2 g
- Sodium 87 mg
- Potassium 186 mg

Roasted Turkey

Discover how Africans roast their turkey, and you'd certainly be so amazed and want to give this a try. Here's an easy recipe that lets you do just that.

Serving Size: 12

Preparation Cooking Time: 4 hours

Ingredients:

- Zest from 1 orange
- ¼ cup berbere spice blend
- 1 cup mayonnaise
- Cooking spray
- 3 cups water
- 1 turkey
- 3 oranges, sliced into wedges
- 1 clove garlic, minced
- 2 tablespoons butter
- Salt to taste

Instructions:

1. Mix the garlic, orange zest and mayonnaise in a bowl.

2. Chill in the refrigerator until ready to use.

3. Preheat your oven to 350 degrees F.

4. Line your roasting pan with foil and spray with oil.

5. Add the water to the roasting pan.

6. Rub all sides of the turkey with the butter.

7. Sprinkle inside and out of the turkey with the salt and spice blend.

8. Insert the orange wedges inside the cavity.

9. Tie the turkey legs together using a kitchen string.

10. Roast in the oven for 1 hour and 30 minutes.

11. Remove the turkey carefully from the oven.

12. Flip and roast for another 45 minutes.

13. Place the turkey on a large cutting board.

14. Let it sit for 20 minutes before slicing.

15. Serve with the reserved orange zest mixture.

Nutrients per Serving:

- Calories 386
- Fat 24.2 g
- Saturated fat 5.6 g
- Carbohydrates 3.7 g
- Fiber 1 g
- Protein 36 g
- Cholesterol 146 mg
- Sugars 2 g
- Sodium 488 mg
- Potassium 342 mg

Roasted Root Veggies

In this quick and simple African recipe, root veggies are seasoned with chermoula and roasted to a golden crisp. Chermoula is a favorite spice blend in Morocco.

Serving Size: 6

Preparation Cooking Time: 1 hour and 15 minutes

Ingredients:

- 3 cloves garlic, minced
- ¼ cup olive oil
- Salt to taste
- 2 teaspoons ground cumin
- 2 teaspoons paprika
- 1 potato, sliced into cubes
- 1 sweet potato, sliced into cubes
- 1 turnip, sliced into cubes
- 1 rutabaga, sliced into cubes
- 2 carrots, sliced into cubes
- 8 oz. butternut squash, sliced into cubes

Instructions:

1. Preheat your oven to 425 degrees F.

2. Add the garlic, oil, salt, cumin and paprika to a food processor.

3. Pulse until smooth.

4. Add the root vegetables in a roasting pan.

5. Toss the root veggies in the garlic oil mixture.

6. Roast the veggies in the oven for 50 minutes.

Nutrients per Serving:

- Calories 234
- Fat 9.9 g
- Saturated fat 1.4 g
- Carbohydrates 34.8 g
- Fiber 6.9 g
- Protein 3.5 g
- Cholesterol 12 mg
- Sugars 10 g
- Sodium 453 mg
- Potassium 808 mg

Citrus Marinade

The mixture you'll make using this recipe can serve as a marinade for chicken, lamb, pork, turkey, or even tofu.

Serving Size: 8

Preparation Cooking Time: 40 minutes

Ingredients:

- 1 tablespoon freshly grated lemon zest

- 2 tablespoons freshly squeezed orange juice

- 2 tablespoons olive oil

- 2 cloves garlic, crushed and minced

- 2 teaspoons ground coriander

- 1 tablespoon ground cumin

- ⅛ teaspoon ground cardamom

- 2 tablespoons freshly squeezed lemon juice

- ¼ teaspoon ground cinnamon

- Salt to taste

- 1 tablespoon freshly grated orange zest

Instructions:

1. Combine all the ingredients in a bowl.

2. Use as marinade for your choice of meat.

3. Cook the meat or poultry according to standard method of preparation.

Nutrients per Serving:

- Calories 41

- Fat 3.8 g

- Saturated fat 0.5 g

- Carbohydrates 1.8 g

- Fiber 0.6 g

- Protein 0.3 g

- Cholesterol 0 mg

- Sugars 1 g

- Sodium 292 mg

- Potassium 115 mg

Pan Roasted Carrots

In this recipe, you'll be seasoning your carrots with a mixture of pumpkin seed, cumin seeds, chickpea flour, pepper, cayenne, and hazelnuts. You can also use this spice blend for other veggies like grilled eggplant, steamed asparagus, or cauliflower steaks.

Serving Size: 6

Preparation Cooking Time: 40 minutes

Ingredients:

- ¼ cup hazelnuts
- 2 teaspoons sesame seeds
- 2 tablespoons pumpkin seeds
- 1 teaspoon cumin seeds
- 1 teaspoon coriander seeds
- 1 tablespoon chickpea flour
- ¼ teaspoon cayenne pepper
- Pepper to taste

Carrots

- 2 tablespoons butter
- 2 lb. carrots, peeled
- Salt to taste
- ¼ cup fresh dill, chopped

Instructions:

1. Put a pan over medium heat.

2. Once hot, add the hazelnuts, sesame seeds, pumpkin seeds, cumin seeds and coriander seeds.

3. Stir and cook for 5 minutes.

4. Transfer to a bowl and let cool.

5. Add the chickpea flour to the pan.

6. Stir until brown.

7. Transfer to another bowl.

8. Place the hazelnut mixture to a blender or spice grinder.

9. Process until fully ground.

10. Add this mixture to the chickpea flour.

11. Stir in the cayenne and pepper.

12. Add the butter to a pan over medium heat.

13. Cook the carrots for 15 minutes.

14. Season the carrots with the salt, dill and hazelnut mixture.

Nutrients per Serving:

- Calories 152

- Fat 9.6 g

- Saturated fat 3 g

- Carbohydrates 15.3 g

- Fiber 4.9 g

- Protein 3.5 g

- Cholesterol 10 mg

- Sugars 7 g

- Sodium 235 mg

- Potassium 520 mg

Lentil Salad

This lentil salad is mixed with carrots and dates. Unlike other salads that are best served immediately after being assembled, this one needs a few minutes to enable the flavors to blend together before serving.

Serving Size: 10

Preparation Cooking Time: 40 minutes

Ingredients:

Dressing

- 1 teaspoon ground cumin
- 1 teaspoon paprika
- ⅓ cup freshly squeezed lemon juice
- Salt and pepper to taste
- ⅓ cup olive oil
- 1 teaspoon lemon zest

Salad

- 1 cup green lentils, rinsed and drained
- Salt to taste
- 1 tablespoon olive oil
- 1 ½ cups onion, diced
- 2 cups carrots, diced
- 12 dates, pitted and chopped
- ½ cup fresh mint leaves, sliced thinly

Instructions:

1. Heat the cumin and paprika in a pan over medium heat for 2 minutes.

2. Transfer to a bowl.

3. Add the lemon juice and season with the salt and pepper.

4. Stir in the oil and lemon zest.

5. Boil the lentil in a pot of water.

6. Reduce heat and simmer for 15 minutes.

7. Season with the salt. Stir.

8. Cook for another 10 minutes.

9. Drain and transfer to a bowl.

10. Pour the oil into a pan over medium heat.

11. Cook the onion and carrots for 10 minutes.

12. Remove from the stove.

13. Stir in the veggies, lentils and dates to the bowl containing the dressing.

14. Mix well.

15. Add the mint leaves before serving.

Nutrients per Serving:

- Calories 250

- Fat 9.3 g

- Saturated fat 1.3 g

- Carbohydrates 38.7 g

- Fiber 8 g

- Protein 6.3 g

- Cholesterol 31 mg

- Sugars 23 g

- Sodium 149 mg

- Potassium 558 mg

Spicy Cod Fillet with Broccolini

Cooking fish fillets like cod in a packet is not only quick and easy; it also means less cleanup. Here's a spicy cod recipe that's best served with cucumbers or carrots.

Serving Size: 4

Preparation Cooking Time: 45 minutes

Ingredients:

- 1 tablespoon peanut oil

- 2 cloves garlic, crushed and minced

- 1 tablespoon ginger, minced

- 4 scallions, chopped

- 2 cups cooked brown rice

- 1 cup broccolini, sliced

- Salt and pepper to taste

- 4 cod fillets

- 2 tablespoons mayonnaise

- 2 tablespoons chili paste

Instructions:

1. Preheat your oven to 450 degrees F.

2. Pour the oil into a pan over medium heat.

3. Cook the garlic, ginger and scallions for 1 minute.

4. Stir in the rice and cook for 1 minute, stirring from time to time.

5. Add ½ cup rice on top of foil sheets.

6. Top the rice with broccolini.

7. Sprinkle with the salt.

8. Top with the fish.

9. Sprinkle the fish with the salt and pepper.

10. In a bowl, mix the mayo and chili paste.

11. Brush the top of the fish with the mixture.

12. Fold the packets and seal.

13. Add the foil packets to the baking pan.

14. Bake in the oven for 15 minutes.

Nutrients per Serving:

- Calories 288

- Fat 6.4 g

- Saturated fat 1.1 g

- Carbohydrates 32.7 g

- Fiber 3 g

- Protein 23.9 g

- Cholesterol 57 mg

- Sugars 3 g

- Sodium 624 mg

- Potassium 574 mg

Moroccan Ratatouille

As you know, ratatouille is a dish that originated in Europe. It is made by combining eggplant, tomatoes, and other veggies. This particular recipe includes cinnamon, a spice popularly used in Moroccan cuisine.

Serving Size: 8

Preparation Cooking Time: 40 minutes

Ingredients:

- 1 eggplant, sliced into cubes
- Salt to taste
- 3 tablespoons olive oil
- 1 teaspoon olive oil
- 1 red bell pepper, diced
- 1 squash, sliced into cubes
- 2 cloves garlic, minced
- 3 tomatoes, diced
- 1 teaspoon sugar
- 1 ¼ teaspoons ground cinnamon
- Pepper to taste

Instructions:

1. Season the eggplant with the salt.

2. Place in the baking pan and let sit for 30 minutes.

3. Rinse and then dry using paper towels.

4. Add 3 tablespoons olive oil to a pan over medium heat.

5. Cook the eggplant, bell pepper and squash for 10 minutes.

6. Transfer to a bowl.

7. Pour the remaining oil to the pan.

8. Add the garlic and tomatoes.

9. Season with the sugar, cinnamon, salt and pepper.

10. Cook for 4 minutes.

11. Add this to the bowl containing the eggplant mixture.

12. Let cool before serving.

Nutrients per Serving:

- Calories 87
- Fat 6.2 g
- Saturated fat 0.9 g
- Carbohydrates 7.7 g
- Fiber 2.8 g
- Protein 1.4 g
- Cholesterol 13 mg
- Sugars 5 g
- Sodium 224 mg
- Potassium 339 mg

Sweet Potato Soup

This recipe is inspired by the traditional peanut soup in West Africa. You can add more chili if you want your soup spicier.

Serving Size: 5

Preparation Cooking Time: 30 minutes

Ingredients:

- 2 sweet potatoes
- 1 tablespoon oil
- 1 onion, chopped
- 1 clove garlic, crushed and minced
- 2 teaspoons fresh ginger, minced
- 4 oz. canned diced green chili
- 3 cups low-sodium tomato juice
- 15 oz. vegetable broth
- 1 teaspoon ground allspice
- ½ cup peanut butter
- Pepper to taste
- Fresh cilantro leaves, chopped

Instructions:

1. Poke the sweet potatoes with fork.

2. Place in the microwave.

3. Microwave on high for 10 minutes.

4. Pour the oil into a pan over medium heat.

5. Cook the onion for 3 minutes.

6. Add the garlic and cook for 1 minute.

7. Add the ginger, green chili, tomato juice, vegetable broth and allspice.

8. Cook for 10 minutes.

9. Slice the sweet potatoes into smaller pieces.

10. Place half of the sweet potatoes to the pot.

11. Add half to the blender.

12. Blend until smooth.

13. Add the pureed sweet potatoes to the pot.

14. Season with the pepper.

15. Sprinkle top with the cilantro and serve in soup bowls.

Nutrients per Serving:

- Calories 302

- Fat 15.8 g

- Saturated fat 2.3 g

- Carbohydrates 28.6 g

- Fiber 5.5 g

- Protein 8.6 g

- Cholesterol 15 mg

- Sugars 12 g

- Sodium 490 mg

- Potassium 862 mg

Chickpea Kidney Bean Salad

Toss chickpeas and kidney beans in a dressing made with lemon juice and cumin. It will definitely be a good addition to your dinner meal.

Serving Size: 10

Preparation Cooking Time: 25 minutes

Ingredients:

- 1 clove garlic, chopped
- Salt to taste
- ½ cup olive oil
- ¼ cup freshly squeezed lemon juice
- ¼ teaspoon ground cinnamon
- 2 tablespoons ground cumin
- 30 oz. kidney beans, rinsed and drained
- 30 oz. canned chickpeas, rinsed and drained
- 1 cup carrot, chopped
- 1 ½ cup parsley, chopped
- ½ cup mint leaves, chopped

Instructions:

1. Mix the garlic and salt in a bowl.

2. Mash together to form a paste.

3. Add the garlic paste to a bowl.

4. Stir in the oil, lemon juice, cinnamon and cumin.

5. Add the rest of the ingredients.

6. Serve right away or chill in the refrigerator for a few minutes before serving.

Nutrients per Serving:

- Calories 221

- Fat 12.2 g

- Saturated fat 1.7 g

- Carbohydrates 22.4 g

- Fiber 7.7 g

- Protein 6.4 g

- Cholesterol 11 mg

- Sugars 1 g

- Sodium 362 mg

- Potassium 372 mg

Kumquat Tagine

Make your tagine (slow-cooked stew, a delicacy in Morroco) with kumquats in this quick and simple recipe.

Serving Size: 6

Preparation Cooking Time: 1 hour and 50 minutes

Ingredients:

- 1 tablespoon olive oil
- 2 onions, sliced thinly
- 1 tablespoon ginger, minced
- 4 cloves garlic, slivered
- 2 lb. chicken thigh fillet, skinned and sliced into cubes
- Salt and pepper to taste
- ¾ teaspoon ground cinnamon
- 1 teaspoon ground cumin
- ⅛ teaspoon ground cloves
- 1 teaspoon ground coriander
- 15 oz. chickpeas, rinsed and drained
- 2 cups kumquats, seeded and chopped
- 1 ½ tablespoons honey
- 14 oz. vegetable broth

Instructions:

1. Preheat your oven to 375 degrees F.

2. Pour the oil into a pan over medium heat.

3. Cook the onion for 4 minutes.

4. Add the ginger and garlic.

5. Cook for 1 minute.

6. Stir in the chicken and cook for 8 minutes.

7. Add the salt, pepper, cinnamon, cumin, cloves and coriander.

8. Cook for 20 seconds.

9. Add the chickpeas, kumquats, honey and broth.

10. Bring to a simmer.

11. Cover the pan.

12. Place it inside the oven.

13. Bake for 1 hour.

Nutrients per Serving:

- Calories 382

- Fat 15 g

- Saturated fat 3.4 g

- Carbohydrates 29.1 g

- Fiber 7.7 g

- Protein 33.2 g

- Cholesterol 101 mg

- Sugars 13 g

- Sodium 542 mg

- Potassium 838 mg

Grilled Steak

Here's the African way of cooking steak on the grill. The steak is seasoned with Moroccan spices and served with sweet potatoes cooked conveniently in a foil packet.

Serving Size: 4

Preparation Cooking Time: 35 minutes

Ingredients:

- 1 teaspoon ground ginger
- 1 teaspoon ground cumin
- 1 teaspoon ground allspice
- ½ teaspoon ground coriander
- ½ teaspoon ground cinnamon
- ½ teaspoon cayenne pepper
- Salt to taste
- 4 strip steaks
- 1 onion, sliced
- 1 lb. sweet potatoes, sliced
- 4 teaspoons oil
- 1 teaspoon orange zest

Instructions:

1. Preheat your grill.

2. In a bowl, mix the ginger, cumin, allspice, coriander, cinnamon, cayenne pepper and salt.

3. Season the steaks with this mixture.

4. Toss the onion and sweet potatoes in this spice mixture.

5. Drizzle with the oil.

6. Sprinkle with the orange zest.

7. Add the sweet potatoes to a foil sheet.

8. Fold the foil and seal the edges.

9. Add the packets to the hottest part of your grill.

10. Cook for 5 minutes per side.

11. Grill the steaks for 4 to 5 minutes per side.

12. Serve the steaks with the sweet potatoes.

Nutrients per Serving:

- Calories 251
- Fat 10.2 g
- Saturated fat 2.4 g
- Carbohydrates 15.4 g
- Fiber 3.2 g
- Protein 23.5 g
- Cholesterol 61 mg
- Sugars 5 g
- Sodium 363 mg
- Potassium 552 mg

North African Turkey

Season your turkey slices with the Berber blend, a popular spice blend in North Africa, and serve with avocado and grapefruit relish.

Serving Size: 6

Preparation Cooking Time: 35 minutes

Ingredients:

- ½ teaspoon ground cinnamon
- 3 grapefruit, peeled and sliced into segments
- 1 avocado, pitted and sliced into cubes
- 1 tablespoon honey
- 1 tablespoon red wine vinegar
- ¼ cup onion, sliced thinly
- 1 tablespoon fresh mint leaves, chopped
- 2 tablespoons fresh cilantro leaves, chopped
- Salt to taste
- ½ teaspoon ground cloves
- ¼ cup chili powder
- ½ teaspoon ground allspice
- 1 ½ lb. turkey cutlets
- 2 teaspoons vegetable oil

Instructions:

1. Preheat your oven to 400 degrees F.

2. Add the grapefruit, avocado, honey, vinegar, onion, mint leaves and cilantro leaves in a bowl.

3. Mix and set aside.

4. In a dish, combine the salt, ground cloves, chili powder, cinnamon and allspice.

5. Season both sides of the turkey using this mixture.

6. Pour the oil into a pan over medium heat.

7. Cook the turkey for 2 minutes per side.

8. Transfer the pan to the oven.

9. Bake for 5 minutes.

10. Serve the turkey with the avocado and grapefruit relish.

Nutrients per Serving:

- Calories 270

- Fat 7.9 g

- Saturated fat 1 g

- Carbohydrates 22.7 g

- Fiber 6.3 g

- Protein 30.6 g

- Cholesterol 45 mg

- Sugars 15 g

- Sodium 355 mg

- Potassium 515 mg

Chicken Tagine with Pomegranates

Here's another way of making chicken tagines. This time, add pomegranates. These don't only infuse the chicken with sweet flavors, but also make the dish more vibrant and colorful.

Serving Size: 4

Preparation Cooking Time: 1 hour and 15 minutes

Ingredients:

- 1 ¼ cups pearl onions
- 1 tablespoon olive oil
- 1 teaspoon ground ginger
- Pepper to taste
- 1 ¼ lb. chicken thigh fillets, skinned
- 1 ½ cups pomegranate juice
- ¾ cup prunes, pitted
- ½ cup dried apricots
- 15 sprigs cilantro, tied with kitchen string
- Salt to taste

Instructions:

1. Preheat your oven to 350 degrees F.

2. Cook the pearl onions for 1 minute.

3. Rinse and drain.

4. Pour the oil into a pan over medium high heat.

5. Add the ginger and season with the pepper.

6. Cook for 1 minute.

7. Cook the chicken and onions for 6 to 8 minutes.

8. Stir in the rest of the ingredients.

9. Simmer for 5 minutes.

10. Transfer the pan to the oven.

11. Bake for 30 minutes.

Nutrients per Serving:

- Calories 432

- Fat 9.4 g

- Saturated fat 2 g

- Carbohydrates 55 g

- Fiber 5.1 g

- Protein 29.6 g

- Cholesterol 133 mg

- Sugars 38 g

- Sodium 433 mg

- Potassium 1186 mg

Pork Ragu

Here's an African version of the much-loved pork ragu dish. Instead of using fatty meat, we opted for lean pork chops to make the dish healthier and lighter as well.

Serving Size: 4

Preparation Cooking Time: 1 hour and 30 minutes

Ingredients:

- 2 ½ teaspoons olive oil, divided
- 2 tablespoons freshly squeezed lemon juice
- 2 teaspoons paprika
- 1 teaspoon ground coriander
- 1 teaspoon ground turmeric
- ½ teaspoon ground cumin
- ¼ teaspoon ground ginger
- Pepper to taste
- 1 ½ pork chops, fat trimmed and sliced into cubes
- 14 oz. low-sodium chicken broth
- 1 onion, chopped
- 2 teaspoons garlic, minced
- ½ cup tomatoes, diced
- 1 cup chickpeas, rinsed and drained
- 1 cup carrots, sliced
- 1 cup butternut squash, sliced into cubes
- 1 tablespoon tomato paste
- ¼ teaspoon hot sauce
- Pinch ground allspice
- Pinch ground cinnamon
- 1 tablespoon freshly grated lemon zest

Instructions:

1. In a bowl, mix ½ teaspoon olive oil, lemon juice, paprika, coriander, turmeric, cumin, ginger and pepper.

2. Add the pork to the bowl.

3. Coat evenly with the mixture.

4. Cover the bowl and refrigerate for 30 minutes.

5. Pour the remaining oil into a pan over medium heat.

6. Cook the pork for 3 minutes or until brown on both sides.

7. Transfer to a plate lined with paper towel.

8. Add the rest of the ingredients to the pot.

9. Bring to a boil.

10. Reduce heat and simmer for 30 minutes.

11. Put the pork back to the pot.

12. Cook for another 3 to 5 minutes and serve.

Nutrients per Serving:

- Calories 280

- Fat 9 g

- Saturated fat 2 g

- Carbohydrates 26.6 g

- Fiber 6.2 g

- Protein 24.2 g

- Cholesterol 57 mg

- Sugars 4 g

- Sodium 488 mg

- Potassium 811 mg

Tunisian Lamb Chops

In Tunisia, lamb chops, as well as other meat, are typically seasoned with a spice blend that includes red pepper flakes, caraway, and cumin. In this recipe, we pair the spiced lamb chops with sautéed chards topped with dates and pine nuts.

Serving Size: 4

Preparation Cooking Time: 35 minutes

Ingredients:

- 2 teaspoons caraway seeds
- 4 teaspoon ground cumin
- ¾ teaspoon red pepper flakes
- Salt and pepper to taste
- 2 lb. lamb chops, fat trimmed
- 4 teaspoons vegetable oil, divided
- ¼ cup dates, chopped
- 1 shallot, chopped
- 1 lb. chard, chopped
- ¼ cup toasted pine nuts

Instructions:

1. Mix the caraway seeds, ground cumin, red pepper flakes, salt and pepper in a bowl.

2. Sprinkle the lamb chops with this mixture.

3. Pour half of the oil into a pan over medium high heat.

4. Cook the lamb chops for 2 minutes per side.

5. Reduce heat and cook for another 3 minutes per side.

6. Transfer the lamb chops to a plate.

7. Pour the remaining oil to the pan.

8. Cook the dates and shallots for 1 minute.

9. Stir in the chard leaves. Cook for 2 minutes.

10. Add the pine nuts and season with the salt.

11. Serve the lamb chops with the sautéed chard.

Nutrients per Serving:

- Calories 323

- Fat 19.5 g

- Saturated fat 3.8 g

- Carbohydrates 8.2 g

- Fiber 3.9 g

- Protein 29.9 g

- Cholesterol 82 mg

- Sugars 2 g

- Sodium 560 mg

- Potassium 1039 mg

Couscous Cauliflower Pilaf

Pilaf is a rice dish that's cooked with meat and veggies. In this recipe, we make one with couscous and cauliflower instead of rice.

Serving Size: 6

Preparation Cooking Time: 25 minutes

Ingredients:

- 1 tablespoon olive oil
- 4 cups cauliflower florets, chopped finely
- Salt to taste
- ¾ cup low-sodium chicken stock
- ¼ cup freshly squeezed orange juice
- ¼ cup currants
- 1 teaspoon orange zest
- ½ cup scallions, chopped
- ⅔ cup couscous (preferably whole-wheat)

Instructions:

1. Pour the oil into a pan over medium heat.

2. Cook the cauliflower for 3 minutes, stirring frequently.

3. Season with the salt.

4. Pour in the stock and orange juice.

5. Add the currants and orange zest.

6. Bring to a boil.

7. Add the scallions and couscous.

8. Remove from the stove.

9. Cover the pan and let sit until liquid has been absorbed.

10. Fluff the couscous using a fork.

Nutrients per Serving:

- Calories 144
- Fat 2.8 g
- Saturated fat 0.4 g
- Carbohydrates 26.8 g
- Fiber 5 g
- Protein 5.6 g
- Cholesterol 13 mg
- Sugars 7 g
- Sodium 291 mg
- Potassium 378 mg

African Chicken Sweet Potato Stew

We tweaked the popular African chicken stew recipe by adding sweet potatoes and tomatoes into the mix. Plus, we serve it on top of couscous mixed with fresh cilantro leaves and lime juice.

Serving Size: 4

Preparation Cooking Time: 45 minutes

Ingredients:

- 1 lb. chicken thigh fillet, skinned and sliced into cubes

- Salt to taste

- 2 teaspoons ground coriander, divided

- 2 tablespoons olive oil, divided

- 1 onion, sliced

- 1 tablespoon ginger, grated

- 1 lb. sweet potato, sliced into cubes

- ¼ cup peanut butter

- 28 oz. canned tomatoes, chopped

- ¼ teaspoon cayenne pepper

- 2 tablespoons lime juice, divided

- 1 ½ cups water

- 1 cup whole-wheat couscous

- 1 cup cilantro leaves, chopped

Instructions:

1. Season the chicken with the salt and half of the coriander.

2. Pour half of the oil into a pan over medium heat.

3. Cook the chicken for 4 minutes per side.

4. Add these to a plate lined with paper towel.

5. Pour the remaining oil to the pan.

6. Cook the onion and ginger for 4 minutes, stirring frequently.

7. Add the sweet potato cubes, peanut butter, tomatoes, cayenne pepper and 1 tablespoon lime juice.

8. Season with the salt and remaining coriander.

9. Bring to a boil.

10. Reduce heat and simmer while covered for 15 minutes. Stir occasionally.

11. Put the chicken back to the pan.

12. Cook for 2 more minutes.

13. Add the water to another pan over medium heat.

14. Bring to a boil.

15. Add the couscous and stir in the remaining lime juice.

16. Remove from the stove.

17. Let sit for 5 minutes.

18. Fluff the couscous using a fork.

19. Add the cilantro.

20. Serve the chicken and potato stew on top of the couscous.

Nutrients per Serving:

- Calories 615

- Fat 24.3 g

- Saturated fat 4.6 g

- Carbohydrates 66.2 g

- Fiber 13.4 g

- Protein 35.1 g

- Cholesterol 76 mg

- Sugars 12 g

- Sodium 457 mg

- Potassium 954 mg

North African Veggie Stew

This vegetable stew is seasoned with the popular Tunisian spice mixture. Since the recipe requires frozen stir-fry veggies, it's convenient to prepare and perfect for a busy weeknight.

Serving Size: 4

Preparation Cooking Time: 35 minutes

Ingredients:

- 2 teaspoons olive oil

- 3 cups frozen stir-fry vegetables

- ½ teaspoon caraway seeds

- 1 teaspoon coriander seeds

- Salt to taste

- ⅛ teaspoon cayenne pepper

- ¼ teaspoon paprika

- 4 cloves garlic, crushed and minced

- 15 oz. canned chickpeas, rinsed and drained

- 28 oz. canned diced tomatoes

- Pepper to taste

- 4 eggs

Instructions:

1. Pour the oil into a pan over medium heat.

2. Cook the vegetables for 5 minutes, stirring from time to time.

3. Place the caraway seeds, coriander seeds and salt in a spice grinder.

4. Grind until powdery.

5. Add to a bowl.

6. Stir in the cayenne pepper and paprika.

7. Add the garlic to the pan.

8. Stir in the spice blend.

9. Cook while stirring for 30 seconds.

10. Stir in the chickpeas and tomatoes.

11. Bring to a boil.

12. Reduce heat and simmer for 15 minutes.

13. Sprinkle with the pepper.

14. Break the eggs carefully on top of the stew.

15. Cover the pan and cook for 5 minutes.

Nutrients per Serving:

- Calories 275

- Fat 9.5 g

- Saturated fat 1.9 g

- Carbohydrates 34.1 g

- Fiber 9.7 g

- Protein 14.9 g

- Cholesterol 186 mg

- Sugars 12 g

- Sodium 613 mg

- Potassium 538 mg

Sweet Spicy Pork Tenderloin

Season slices of pork tenderloin with a combination of sweet and spicy flavors and serve with zucchini and freekeh.

Serving Size: 4

Preparation Cooking Time: 30 minutes

Ingredients:

- 3 tablespoons olive oil, divided
- 1 cup freekeh
- 2 cups water
- Salt and pepper to taste
- ¼ teaspoon saffron
- 1 lb. baby zucchini
- 4 slices pork tenderloin, trimmed
- 1 ½ teaspoons harissa
- 2 tablespoons honey
- 2 teaspoons garlic, crushed and minced

Instructions:

1. Preheat your oven to 425 degrees F.

2. Mix 1 tablespoon olive oil, freekeh, water, salt, pepper and saffron in a pan over medium heat.

3. Bring to a boil.

4. Reduce heat and simmer for 20 minutes.

5. Coat the squash with the 1 tablespoon oil.

6. Season with the salt and pepper.

7. Sprinkle both sides of the pork tenderloin with the salt and pepper.

8. In a bowl, mix the harissa, honey and garlic.

9. Pour the remaining oil to a pan over medium high heat.

10. Cook the pork tenderloin for 3 minutes or until brown.

11. Flip and brush with the honey and harissa mixture.

12. Sprinkle the squash around the pork tenderloin.

13. Roast in the oven for 10 minutes.

14. Serve the pork and squash with the freekeh.

Nutrients per Serving:

- Calories 444
- Fat 14.8 g
- Saturated fat 2.4 g
- Carbohydrates 46.2 g
- Fiber 9.1 g
- Protein 32.2 g
- Cholesterol 74 mg
- Sugars 12 g
- Sodium 711 mg
- Potassium 753 mg

Moroccan Chicken with Peach Salsa

Previously, we learned how to make a citrus marinade that can be used to flavor up chicken, turkey, lamb, or pork. In this recipe, we use this marinade for grilled chicken and make a sweet and spicy peach salsa to accompany it.

Serving Size: 8

Preparation Cooking Time: 5 hours and 40 minutes

Ingredients:

- 10 to 12 tablespoons citrus marinade

- 8 chicken thighs, skinned

- 1 onion, chopped

- 1 lb. peaches, sliced in half and pitted

- 1 tablespoon olive oil

- 2 tablespoons fresh cilantro leaves, chopped

- 1 jalapeño pepper, chopped

- 2 tablespoons freshly squeezed lime juice

- 1 teaspoon freshly grated lime zest

- Salt to taste

Instructions:

1. Marinate the chicken in the citrus mixture for 4 hours in the refrigerator, covered.

2. Preheat your grill.

3. Brush the onion and peaches with the olive oil.

4. Grill the peaches for 2 to 3 minutes per side, and the onions 5 minutes per side.

5. Transfer these to a cutting board and let cool.

6. Once cool enough to handle, chop.

7. Transfer to a bowl.

8. Stir in the fresh cilantro leaves, jalapeño pepper, lime juice, lime zest and salt. Set aside.

9. Grill the chicken for 10 to 12 minutes per side or until fully cooked.

10. Serve with the peach salsa.

Nutrients per Serving:

- Calories 257
- Fat 10.9 g
- Saturated fat 2.4 g
- Carbohydrates 8.3 g
- Fiber 1.5 g
- Protein 30.5 g
- Cholesterol 116 mg
- Sugars 6 g
- Sodium 388 mg
- Potassium 431 mg

Lamb Tagine with Rhubarb

Rhubarb adds savory flavors to your lamb stew. If lamb is not available, you can also make use of pork shoulder. Serve this with couscous or brown rice.

Serving Size: 6

Preparation Cooking Time: 3 hours and 30 minutes

Ingredients:

- 2 lb. lamb leg, sliced into cubes
- Salt and pepper to taste
- 3 tablespoons butter
- 4 cups onions, sliced
- 2 cinnamon sticks
- 2 cloves garlic, sliced thinly
- 1 teaspoon ground ginger
- ½ teaspoon cayenne pepper
- 1 teaspoon cumin seeds
- 28 oz. canned diced tomatoes (unsalted)
- 2 cups reduced-sodium chicken stock
- 3 cups rhubarb, chopped
- 3 tablespoons brown sugar
- ½ cup raisins
- Parsley, chopped

Instructions:

1. Preheat your oven to 325 degrees F.

2. Sprinkle both sides of the lamb with the salt and pepper.

3. Add the butter to a pot over medium heat.

4. Cook the onions for 7 minutes, stirring occasionally.

5. Add the cinnamon sticks, garlic, ground ginger, cayenne pepper and cumin seeds.

6. Cook for 1 minute.

7. Pour in the tomatoes and stock.

8. Stir in the rhubarb, brown sugar and raisins.

9. Increase heat and bring to a boil.

10. Add the lamb to the stew.

11. Cover the pot.

12. Transfer the pot to the oven.

13. Bake for 2 hours.

14. Set the oven temperature to 425 degrees F.

15. Remove the cover and bake for another 40 minutes.

16. Season with the salt and pepper.

17. Garnish with the parsley before serving.

Nutrients per Serving:

- Calories 366
- Fat 13.8 g
- Saturated fat 6.4 g
- Carbohydrates 33.2 g
- Fiber 5.2 g
- Protein 29.8 g
- Cholesterol 94 mg
- Sugars 21 g
- Sodium 458 mg
- Potassium 1047 mg

Stuffed Peppers

Stuffed peppers are a popular appetizer anywhere in the world. In this recipe, we make it the way it is made in African cuisine.

Serving Size: 2

Preparation Cooking Time: 30 minutes

Ingredients:

- 2 large bell peppers, tops sliced off

- Water

- 2 cloves garlic, crushed and minced

- 8 oz. lean ground beef

- ¼ cup currants

- ½ teaspoon ground cinnamon

- 1 teaspoon ground cumin

- 1 cup cooked brown rice

- 1 ¼ cup reduced-sodium vegetable juice, divided

- Salt and pepper to taste

- ½ teaspoon orange zest

- 2 tablespoons fresh mint leaves, chopped

Instructions:

1. Add the peppers to a microwave-safe dish.

2. Fill the dish with water.

3. Microwave on high for 3 minutes.

4. Drain the peppers.

5. In a pan over medium heat, cook the garlic and beef for 5 minutes, stirring frequently.

6. Add the currants.

7. Season with the cinnamon and cumin.

8. Cook while stirring for 1 minute.

9. Add the rice and cook for 30 seconds.

10. Remove from the stove.

11. Pour in ¼ cup vegetable juice.

12. Add the salt, pepper, orange zest and mint leaves.

13. Stuff the beef mixture into the peppers.

14. Drizzle with the remaining vegetable juice.

15. Microwave on high for 2 minutes.

Nutrients per Serving:

- Calories 469

- Fat 12.1 g

- Saturated fat 4.2 g

- Carbohydrates 52.2 g

- Fiber 7.8 g

- Protein 36.7 g

- Cholesterol 87 mg

- Sugars 22 g

- Sodium 483 mg

- Potassium 1423 mg

Scallops Stew

In this fuss-free stew recipe, scallops are cooked in white wine and tomatoes and seasoned with herbs like tarragon. The result is an outstanding seafood stew everyone will surely be fond of. Serve with crusty bread and green salad.

Serving Size: 4

Preparation Cooking Time: 35 minutes

Ingredients:

- 1 lb. sea scallops
- Salt to taste
- 2 teaspoons olive oil
- ½ cup onion, sliced thinly
- 2 cloves garlic, sliced thinly
- 2 celery stalks, sliced thinly
- ¼ cup white wine
- 1 cup cherry tomatoes, sliced in half
- 8 oz. baby potatoes, sliced
- ¼ teaspoon saffron threads
- ¾ cup tomato juice
- 1 cup low-sodium chicken stock
- 2 teaspoons fresh tarragon, chopped

Instructions:

1. Dry the scallops using a paper towel.

2. Season both sides of the scallops with the salt.

3. Pour the oil into a pan over medium high heat.

4. Cook the scallops for 2 minutes per side.

5. Transfer these to a plate.

6. Cook the onion, garlic and celery for 2 minutes.

7. Pour in the wine.

8. Simmer for 1 minute.

9. Add the cherry tomatoes, baby potatoes and saffron threads.

10. Pour in the tomato juice and chicken stock.

11. Bring to a boil.

12. Reduce heat, cover and simmer for 13 to 15 minutes.

13. Add the scallops back to the pan.

14. Season with the tarragon.

15. Cover the pan and cook for another 3 minutes.

16. Serve warm.

Nutrients per Serving:

- Calories 179

- Fat 3.2 g

- Saturated fat 0.5 g

- Carbohydrates 18.5 g

- Fiber 2.2 g

- Protein 16.6 g

- Cholesterol 27 mg

- Sugars 4 g

- Sodium 848 mg

- Potassium 802 mg

Conclusion

There are too many things to love about African cuisine that you'd probably take a long time to mention them all.

Now that you've tried some of the recipes in this book, and you know that African cuisine deserves more attention than it gets.

Serve these dishes to your family and friends, so you can enjoy together the beauty, flavor, and aroma of Africa.

About the Author

A native of Albuquerque, New Mexico, Sophia Freeman found her calling in the culinary arts when she enrolled at the Sante Fe School of Cooking. Freeman decided to take a year after graduation and travel around Europe, sampling the cuisine from small bistros and family owned restaurants from Italy to Portugal. Her bubbly personality and inquisitive nature made her popular with the locals in the villages and when she finished her trip and came home, she had made friends for life in the places she had visited. She also came home with a deeper understanding of European cuisine.

Freeman went to work at one of Albuquerque's 5-star restaurants as a sous-chef and soon worked her way up to head chef. The restaurant began to feature Freeman's original dishes as specials on the menu and soon after, she began to write e-books with her recipes. Sophia's dishes mix local flavours with European inspiration making them irresistible to the diners in her restaurant and the online community.

 Freeman's experience in Europe didn't just teach her new ways of cooking, but also unique methods of presentation. Using rich sauces, crisp vegetables and meat cooked to perfection, she creates a stunning display as well as a delectable dish. She has won many local awards for her cuisine and she continues to delight her diners with her culinary masterpieces.

Author's Afterthoughts

I want to convey my big thanks to all of my readers who have taken the time to read my book. Readers like you make my work so rewarding and I cherish each and every one of you.

Grateful cannot describe how I feel when I know that someone has chosen my work over all of the choices available online. I hope you enjoyed the book as much as I enjoyed writing it.

Feedback from my readers is how I grow and learn as a chef and an author. Please take the time to let me know your thoughts by leaving a review on Amazon so I and your fellow readers can learn from your experience.

My deepest thanks,

Sophia Freeman

https://sophia.subscribemenow.com/

Printed in Great Britain
by Amazon

44638923R00104